EVERYTHING THAT RISES

ALSO BY JOSEPH STROUD

Of This World: New and Selected Poems
Country of Light
Below Cold Mountain
Signatures
In the Sleep of Rivers

CHAPBOOKS AND LIMITED EDITIONS

Diversion
Poetics
My Diamond Sutra
Night Psalms
Kingdom Come
Ukiyo-e
Three Odes of Pablo Neruda
Burning the Years
Unzen

EVERYTHING THAT RISES

JOSEPH STROUD

COPPER CANYON PRESS
PORT TOWNSEND, WASHINGTON

Cover art: Leo Kenney, *Fire Sign*, 1972. Gouache on Chinese paper,
27 x 10 inches. Copyright William Merchant Pease, Literary Executor and
Attorney for the Estate of Leo Kenney; Courtesy of the Estate of
Caryl Roman.

Copper Canyon Press is in residence at Fort Worden State Park in Port
Townsend, Washington, under the auspices of Centrum. Centrum is a gath-
ering place for artists and creative thinkers from around the world, students
of all ages and backgrounds, and audiences seeking extraordinary cultural
enrichment.

LIBRARY OF CONGRESS CATALOGING-IN-PUBLICATION DATA
Names: Stroud, Joseph, 1943– author.
Title: Everything that rises / Joseph Stroud.
Description: Port Townsend, Washington : Copper Canyon Press, [2019]
Identifiers: LCCN 2019018418 | ISBN 9781556595646 (paperback)
Classification: LCC PS3569.T73 A6 2019 | DDC 811/.54—dc23
LC record available at https://lccn.loc.gov/2019018418

9 8 7 6 5 4 3 2 FIRST PRINTING

COPPER CANYON PRESS
Post Office Box 271
Port Townsend, Washington 98368
www.coppercanyonpress.org

to the memory of Roberta McNamara Stroud

for Miette Elle Sparrow Scott

everything that rises must converge

PIERRE TEILHARD DE CHARDIN / FLANNERY O'CONNOR

CONTENTS

2 STRINGS

PART ONE
MY DIAMOND SUTRA

Stone Sutra

My sutra is silence. Solitude. Holding
a stone in my hand. A hard river stone
worn smooth by water — what a river
does to granite over time. Holding
quietude in my hand. Holding silence
like a rock. Elemental. Adamantine.

Homage to Wang Wei

A Chinese scroll painting the length of a wall,
brushed-ink mountain ranges with pine forests,
clouds drifting over peaks, a waterfall tumbling
down a cliff, and off to the side, a little bridge
over a creek, on it a figure, hardly noticeable,
crossing over, about to disappear in the mists.

Frost

It was a winter dusk and the crows
were calling your name, so you rose
from your life, you left everything,
your past, your home, you had another
place to be going beyond the snowy fields
filling with night inside your poem.

Thou Gavest It to Me
from the Foundation of the World

I had no words when my mother died.
I had no poem, no vision, no way out of grief.
So I turned to Emily: *The great mission of pain*
had been ratified—cultivated to tenderness
by persistent sorrow, so that a larger mother
died [O Mother!] *than had she died before.*

At the Center of Light in Michoacán

Every noon the Tarascan and her daughter
walked through the broken streets near the river
carrying a tin bucket filled with steaming tamales —
and every noon I bought some, unwrapped the husks
and broke them open, eating the sweet white corn
near thousands of monarchs wintering in the trees.

Hózh'q

Certainly the highlands of Todos Santos Cuchumatán.
And Bali near Lake Agung. And the Yorkshire Dales.
And the village of Ólimbos above the Aegean. But also
an autumn morning, kneeling over an icy stream
in Kings Canyon, cupping cold water in my hands,
kneeling into the moment, into the diamond of my life.

Turning on the Radio, News of Iraq, Summer 2003

I'm driving the twenty-five miles from Markleeville
into Minden, down 88 through the Carson Valley plain,
half a dozen magpies flocking in a hay field just plowed,
two horses flicking their tails and running in a pasture,
Jobs Peak and Jobs Sister looming over all as I struggle
to keep my mind clear in the radio's ambush of horror.

Flash Point

Out the cabin window a coyote streaks past,
our eyes for an instant locking — *electric* —
then he's down the trail, and then he's gone.
All morning I feel a wild shimmering —
in windows, pine needles — a presence
in my mind — as in all things fiercely *seen*.

Laos, Plain of Jars, in the Shadow of War

My left boot was streaked with blood
leaking from under my pant leg,
but I felt no pain as I rolled up the khaki
and there as big as a thumb and fastened
just below my knee was a jungle leech
black and swollen as the tongue of Satan.

In the Golden Triangle

One night I listened to a Kang shaman chanting
over a sick child. She died at dawn as the farmers
were leaving to tend poppies with blossoms
the size of fists. In the secret American war over
the next range, Thunderchiefs dropped napalm
erupting in blossoms as large as a village.

Once

in memory of Paul Pera

I remember when happiness was a Berkeley
summer evening under a live oak, with a glass
of wine, reading aloud from our first poems,
the words lit from within, like stars, like notes
from Laurindo Almeida's Spanish guitar
and Salli Terri singing "Carmen Carmela."

Homage to the Makar

I think of George Mackay Brown in Stromness
sometime in the Seventies, waking after a night
of hard drinking, sitting in his kitchen with light
slashing through storm clouds, his pen in hand,
hungover, the empty page before him, and then
in a shaking scrawl — *I lean into the sun's loom.*

Epithalamion

A fragment of Sappho [...*as long as*...] and we'll
never know the context, though maybe it was
summer on Lesbos, fields of barley, the sun
threshing the sea, stone terraces the color
of honey, and someone singing... *for as long
as you wish*... to the dancing groom and bride.

Portuguese Bend, Palos Verdes, 1959

after Sappho

Remember that night below
the palisades when the moon
came apart in the waves like a pearl
breaking open and the stars fell
in a rain of fire as we opened to
each other that once and only time

Heart Attack in an Oregon Forest

On your cellphone you tried to direct
the sheriff to where you were along the river.
Just before he found you he could almost hear
his own voice through the phone still held
in your hand, his voice calling your name,
asking directions from the dead.

About Suffering, the Old Masters
Were Never Wrong

Hemingway in Key West received a package
from his mother, and opening it he found
a birthday cake, along with a silver Colt .22,
a pistol Hemingway knew well, the very gun
his father had put to his own head, the one
that rang out for years over the life of his son.

Reading Lorca for the First Time

His poems were wild horses
on the bank of a river. I was on
the other side, on my knees, bringing
water to my mouth with folded hands.
I loved seeing those horses. They had come
from so far. And no one had ever ridden them.

The Great Crystal

I think of Rexroth those final days, alone
in his study, listening to arias, the voices
washing over him for the last time, his eyes
streaming tears, his heart failing, his mind
as clear as the crystal paperweight on his desk
atop a Chinese poem a thousand years old.

Running the Rapids

Yang Wan-li, drunk on wine in his little boat,
enters the rapids unaware, spinning and bobbing
and tossed about like a doll, almost falling out,
raises his arms, gives everything over to *whatever!*
laughing, thrilled — only later downriver, sober
and trembling, does he realize what he's been over.

Postcard to William Carlos Williams

Well, Bill, I think things just might be okay,
because the mockingbird singing like crazy
on top of the loquat tree is holding his own
against the screeching jay from down the block,
puffed up and strutting around in his mohawk,
thinking he's singing, but mostly it's just *squawk.*

Larkinism

Philip Larkin said he didn't understand poets
who went around the universities explaining
in intimate detail how they wrote poems —
It's like going round explaining how
you sleep with your wife — and in America
they probably get paid for that as well.

I Saw Whitman and Ginsberg Yesterday

They weren't in the bookstore among the books,
they were on the freeway, in a Thunderbird,
top down, pedal to the metal, beards streaming
in the wind — our old fathers — heading out,
no special place to go — just open spaces
on the open road, Bo Diddley on the radio.

Imagining (Poetry)

for Michael, my twin brother

We strung fifty feet of string between two cans,
my brother on one side of the fence, me on the other,
he talked into his can as I held mine to my ear,
and then we would switch, whispering to each other
our secrets, what we told no one else, hearing
at each end only what we might imagine.

Oppen / Praxis

Write it down lucidly. Say what happened
in a way that makes it happen again. In us.
You don't have to make things up. You don't
have to wear jewelry. No need for hyperbole.
Clarity and accuracy honor the reader.
Don't muddy the waters. Do rock the boat.

The Perfection of Craft

The great blue heron stalks among reeds,
stops — *alert* — then stabs its beak, flings
into the air a roiling snake, and catches it,
tosses it again, the snake not knowing
what on earth, caught once more, head first,
still alive, slithering down the heron's throat.

Homage to Jean Follain

Provence, a field of sunflowers
all facing the course of the sun,
and at the edge of a path a boy
walks into them and disappears.
What do I know, what does any
one know of any given moment?

Mosul

Tell us of the dominion of bees and the palace
of honey, tell us of the throne of light inside
the honeycomb, the ingots of amber honey.
Tell us, for we've been listening to the days
burning down, to news of all the bodies
dug up in the marshes outside of town.

Trakl, Gródek, 1914

This is the day when there is nothing more
to say, when a man puts a pistol to his head.
This is the day when the bells are ringing
over all the dead, when the milk-white
porcelain bowl on the table looks like
a skull, and nothing anywhere is singing.

Perhaps *You* Know

Turning a corner in Mexico one day I came
upon the severed head of a steer in the street,
its horns curving down toward the nostrils
that seemed to breathe, its eyes beginning
to glaze. This was a morning in Apatzingán,
and one more thing I've failed to understand.

High Noon in Apatzingán

A boy squats next to an empty fountain.
Two old men in cowboy hats and cracked boots
play a game with bottle caps on a board
so weathered all the black squares are white.
The boy pulls the legs off one side of a beetle
and watches as it hobbles around in a circle.

Miss Emily

Don't be fooled. In her poems
there's a blade as keen as the razors
strapped to the spurs of cocks who
burst together in a rage of feathers
a foot above the dirt and one of them
is dead before it hits the ground.

Among the Ruins

Digging into the poem with bare hands
you feel something round and hard
and clearing away the words you find
the upturned head of your father
surfacing from some other world
staring at you as if *you* were dead

Homage to the Water Ouzel

Times you get so far down into pain all you
can do is think of the ouzel in the middle of winter,
a stream running through patches of ice, and into
this aching cold water the little bird plunges
and walks the bottom just trying to stay alive.
Imagine that. *Jesus Christ.* Try to imagine that.

How I Got Over

One morning below Desolation an owl
broke from a pine tree — startling me —
a great horned owl — wingspan as wide
as my arms — it rose from the limbs —
as if lifting me — *mercy* — as if bearing me
out of sorrow — winging over the trees

Between Worlds

There are those moments when you're suspended
between the dream and the waking world, between
the dream-self and the flesh-self — this morning
for instance, talking with my mother, our happiness,
my amazement as the room flared sun-bright,
and my mother, dead forty years, dissolved in light.

Shiva as a Wind in the Cottonwoods

Maybe those cottonwoods, and the little stream,
and the silver threads of a web, and spring sunlight,
have a purpose, a reason for being, and nobody,
this is the truth, nobody knows what it is, though
all of us have wondered — *O World of Forms* —
to be in this body this brief and only time.

Working on My Headstone, Charlotteville, Tobago

The little goat who followed me each morning
has disappeared. No more bells. No more
crazy love. Just this jungle writhing with vines
where insects seethe. No more little goat.
Sweet one. Now it's time to be alone, to clear
away the spoilage, chisel the words into stone.

The Quiet Masters

And then there are those poets whose poems disappear
as soon as you've read them, and you can't say what
the poem was about, just that you find in yourself
a disturbance, a premonition, as the poem descends
through your life, like a depth charge, set to detonate
only under enough pressure of time and sorrow.

Remember This, Sappho Said

When the time comes and Death leads you
to the Underworld where you will wander
bodiless among the shades, remember that
among the living you were once offered love —
you, with your great pride and haughty disdain,
remember love once was offered, and you refrained.

My Diamond Sutra

And all those days, the Tehachapis, cottonwoods
in the crown of summer, those burnished seasons
with friends, wine and laughter, the sweet embrace
of this world, all those days, where are they, what's
become of them, those loves, dreams, those dragon
boats of poems, set on fire, pushed into the stream.

PART TWO
STRINGS

Under Orion

March 20, 2003

Shay Creek
late night
Orion rising
as I read Hitomaro's
thirteen-hundred-year-old poem
of tenderness
for this forsaken
ill-loved world
a poem where he sits
among the ruins
of Otsu palace
drinking
cold rice wine
in a night
surrounded by war
hundreds of miles
from his wife
and child
drinking cup
after cup
sitting in the great hall
of night
under the rising sword
of Orion

Exchange

after Saussure

I hand over
a bill
engraved with
the image of a king
in silk and pearls
on one side
on the other
an orchid
and elephant
under teak trees
these
I hand to a man
who smiles
and gives me
in return
an actual
rose-hued
mango
and a river
swallow
alive
in a small
bamboo cage

Uprooting a Sunflower in Winter

in memory of Seamus Heaney

Grab the stem close to the earth,
grip it with both hands, pull slowly,
don't wrench, don't yank or jerk it,
pull it slowly up, feel the tight roots
unloosening, listen to the sound
it makes coming out of the ground
where it drank deep, pulling up
grains of water into its leaves
feeding on sunlight and the great
crowned head clustered with seeds
drooped earthward under the weight
of birds with their evolved beaks
plucking seeds each with a kernel
of sunflower nestled within

The Summer of Walking Through the Dead

The quickest way to the dime store
was across the park and through
the cemetery then down the gully
along the creek to the fishing hole
that held no fish then up to the town
clock frozen at 1:22 and you were
in front of the bakery and just
next door was the dime store
where with a nickel from Grandma
you were rich beyond measure
for a penny could buy a jawbreaker
the size of a boulder which is what
we called a giant marble but this one
you could put in your mouth
and suck on as you walked back
the way you came and by the time
you reached the cemetery the hard
rock candy had dissolved
to the size of a BB and soon enough
there was nothing left in your mouth
but sweetness walking among
the graves reading the strange
names of the dead with a few coins
jingling in your pocket as you
made your way back to Branch Street
through a summer as forever
as the forever of your childhood

The Spirit Will Not Go Back into Flesh

in memory of Linda Kitz

All life is incarnation
for look what death leaves
a body bereft of *everything*
Buddhists say the spirit remains
a presence for three days
around the corpse
but I had no sense of it
in Linda's room
when the lama clapped his hands
over her body
so her spirit would know we were there
clapped his hands three times
sharply
as I did in Hanoi once
in a Buddhist garden
kneeling over a pond
clapping
and koi rose to the surface
like spirits
their mouths opening
into an element
where they could not
live

Distances

What is the distance between fire in the Sweetwaters
and rain in the Mojave
Between a riverbed in the Tehachapis
and a slow journey up the Irrawaddy to Mandalay
What is the distance
between blue iris in the Forest of Nisene Marks
and blue flames of flowers in the *Très Riches Heures*
Between the taste of her mouth on a beach in Mazatlán
and a taste of the white honey of Auvergne
How do you measure the distance
between the young lovers asleep in a farmhouse
arms around each other in the morning light
and the old man returning in memory fifty years after
looking down on them — looking across a distance
measured by all the mornings of his world

The Lost World

In T'ao Ch'ien's poem a fisherman goes far
into the wilderness and comes upon a cave,
which he enters and walks through
until he comes out into another world,
a landscape of tilled fields with gardens
and thatched huts and people going about
their lives with a serene contentment,
and they invite the fisherman into their homes,
feed him, give him wine, question him
about the other world they had left
centuries before, trying to escape famine and war
to settle in this hidden place, and the fisherman
tells them what he knows of history,
of changing dynasties, rebellions, wars.
When he turns to leave they ask that he
not tell those out there where he had been,
so the fisherman goes back into his world,
with the story of this unknown place,
a country so many have been searching for,
a lost world not even the fisherman
or T'ao Ch'ien could find again.

Tarantula

Below Solomon Ridge
walking out of the desert
and crossing the road —
a tarantula
the size of my hand.
When I approach,
it stops, rears up,
feels the air with its front legs,
its body covered in silky hair,
face,
if you could call it a face,
glittering with eyes.
I kneel
and it turns to follow the shadow
of my hand,
a little dance
before pouncing
on the twig I hold before it.
It seems curious, intelligent,
looking up as if wondering
what happens now, what will you do,
who in this world *are* you.
Then its fangs
click open.
I stand, take a step back.
It watches, unmoving,
waiting inside its own
arachnid time
before continuing on,
touching the ground delicately
with each tip of its eight legs,

heading out into the Mojave,
into the creosote and Joshua,
walking like a hand
dancing over fire,
walking carefully
into a life
we will never know
and now disappearing
into a world
where we cannot go.

The Bear

There's a black bear up behind the cabin
peering around a sugar pine, looking down
on me looking up at him, the forest quiet,
as if waiting — the bear is *snuffling*, trying
to pick up a scent. I begin to slowly
walk toward him — pause — watch the bear
who now seems curious about what *I* might be —
mouth open, he's making a *whuffing* sound,
rises on his hind legs, drops back to all fours,
hesitates, as I gaze up the slope toward him,
a young bear, maybe two hundred pounds,
amber fur, narrow snout, and now
I can smell *him* — acrid, musky — the bear
looks at me, maybe I'm his first human,
he's not a campground bear, one of those
bears who peel open cars, rip apart coolers,
bears with little fear of humans — this bear
is backcountry wild, and needs to know what
to fear — come hunting season around here,
a curious bear is a dead bear — so I fling my arms
in the air — clap and yell — he *whuffs*
and goes crashing uphill through brush
and is gone. I stand a long while listening.
The forest goes back to being a forest —
a goshawk glides under the canopy of trees,
a ground squirrel scurries for its burrow,
and all the needles of the pines, backlit
by the sun, quiver and shine.

Animal Fair, 1950

> *I went to the animal fair*
> *the birds and the beasts were there*

Traditional folk song

And then my father and mother
are locked in a metal cage
and they rise into the sky
in a great wheel
going up
and up and around
and back down
would they ever return
to earth
would they ever
wheeling through the sky
come back to me
they wave as they pass by
they seem happy
then the wheel
with its flashing lights
slows to a stop
a man unlocks the cage
pulls back the bar
and my mother and father
step
onto the ground
and we walk back
among the cages
of the birds and the beasts
we stop at a booth
where a man sells chameleons

small green lizards
alive
each clasped in a collar
fastened
to a tiny chain
which I pin to my shirt
and we walk
through the fair
past tents with posters
showing a woman
swallowing a sword
a man tying himself
into knots
and the world's smallest horse
standing
in the palm of a hand
I hold in my hands
the hands of my mother and father
walking between them
out of the fair
out of my fear
and we drive
the long road home
the chameleon
still pinned to my chest
changing
from brown to green to gold
as if trying to match
the color of my heart

Kingdom Come

to the spirit of Francisco José de Goya y Lucientes

GOLD DAY

Walk the East Fork
of the Carson
below Leviathan
cutthroat streaming
in the river's jade
wind skirl
and green flash of kingfisher
thistles
spiking bloodstars
on thin stalks
fireweed
blazing pentecost
sun
scattering ingots
over gold
shoals

BAJA

Diamonds down
its back a lyre snake
coils under ocotillo
next to a skullhead
cholla on whose spine
a shrike has spiked
a scorpion as the lyre
flicks its tongue
into air near the caracara
folding its wings
over a dog
dead on the highway
asphalt shimmering
heat waves
where a truck in the distance
disappears

SPECTER

Goya's spirit
rises at noon
in the plaza
like a ghost
catching fire
spirit the color
of sun
and crimson leaves
whirling
in a dust devil
leaves swirling
around nothing
gusting up
in the heat
then collapsing
at your feet

ENTROPY

The cow
dead in a field
its belly unseamed
worms seething inside
a sound
like the machinery
of the sun
eating through marble
burrowing into Rome
into the Forum
the Pantheon in ruins
everywhere columns
collapsing
everything disassembling
coming apart
in the great engine of light

EEL FISHING ON A FOGGY SWEDISH BEACH

Pulled from the sea
the severed head
of a horse
eye sockets
runneling with eels
caught by a fisherman
who stuffs them
in a sack
and walks
down the beach
over sand
the color of fog
the color of sea
disappearing
into where the world
used to be

RELIC

In Úbeda a priest
asks do you want
to go down
under the altar
do you want
to enter the crypt
to witness
the miraculous
preserved hand
of Saint John of the Cross
asks are you
a Believer
would you like
to touch
maybe kiss
a finger

INTELLIGENT DESIGN

A summer pond
choked with waterweeds
algae spuming in shallows
horsehair worms & spawn-froth
leeches & water scorpions
predacious water beetles
assassin flies flying in the air
flame skimmers & meadowhawks
breeze rattling bulrushes
and attached to a cattail
the exoskeleton of a naiad
its split empty husk
while above it the naked
fleshed-out changeling
engorged with blood
pulses in the sun

REVELATION

Among rushes
below the levee
an egret with eyes gone
and gone the luster
of feathers its chest
splayed open
sunlight paging
through the changes
Book of the Future
there by the river
each cell
a burned-out star
ghost city
within the body
shambles
of New Jerusalem

PART THREE

NIGHT THOUGHTS WHILE TRAVELING

Copa

after Virgil

in memory of Helen Waddell

Come in, traveler,
sit down and rest yourself.
The arbor is cool here
shaded with vines and leaves.
You can hear the sound
of someone playing a flute
in the grotto. Come in.
In here's a woman
with her hair in ribbons,
swaying, half drunk,
moving her body to music.
Come in. You're tired,
and it's so hot out there
in the dust and Roman sun.
Here, drink this wine.
There are garlands here,
violets and meadow rue
picked near the bend of the river
where Miranda gathers them
in a green willow basket.
Here are plates of cheese
the farmers dry in baskets
woven from rushes.
Here are sweet plums,
berries, clusters of grapes,
green cucumbers that hang
from the trellis.
Come in, friend.

Look how your little burro
is tired and sad.
Spare the little burro!
It's so hot out there
where cicadas shrill in the trees
and lizards skitter in weeds
looking for shade.
Sit here, lie still,
quench yourself with drink,
raise your glass
and gaze through it,
see the world take on
the color of tawny wine.
What could be sweeter
than to lie under these vines
entwined in a woman's arms?
As for those old moralists
with their dismissive looks —
what do they prefer:
ashes?
or this wine, these flowers?
So my friend,
forget about tomorrow.
Raise your glass.
Drink the wine.
Can't you hear Death
breathing in your ear?
Live, he whispers. *Live.*
For I am coming.

Catullus: Two Poems

To Manius —

Friend, you ask me for songs and love poems
because you are so unhappy. Let me tell you
how it is with me —

                      Once, many years ago
when I first entered the garden and strolled
through its mornings learning how to sing
Love's songs, my life was filled with light,
brimming with poems. But all that ended
when my brother died —

                    Brother!
Your death took away all my happiness,
left our house in ruins. You are gone.
And gone with you the joy you made
of our days.

                   Thus, Manius,
memory cheats me of the present, and I have
no songs, no poems, to offer you.

CI

Brother —
I have traveled all through this world,
and my journeys have brought me here
to this grief before your grave, here
where I scatter words like ashes over your dust.
Death has torn you from me. And so
I've come to perform the ancient ritual.
Accept these poor offerings, these words
mixed with tears. In this life, my brother,
we will never meet again. This farewell —
is forever.

Tu Fu: Eight Poems

NIGHT OF FULL MOON

This night's full moon also rises over Fu-chou
where my wife in her chamber watches it alone
I think of my children with sorrow
too young to understand why I am in Ch'ang-an
My wife's hair is scented with night mist
her arms cold as jade in the moonlight
When will we be together again
gazing at the moon drying our tears

SPRING SCENE

The empire may fall, rivers and mountains remain
Spring in the ravaged city, grass and trees flourish
but in these troubled times flowers seem to weep
I think of my family, birds startle my heart
Beacon fires have been burning for months
I would give a fortune for any news from home
My hair has grown so thin from worried scratching
soon there won't be enough to stick a hatpin in!

THINKING OF MY BROTHERS ON A MOONLIT NIGHT

War drums on the watchtower keep the roads empty
Autumn, the sound of a lone goose on the frontier
Tonight begins the season when dew turns to frost
The moon here shines as it used to in my homeland
My brothers are scattered in different directions
I have no way to know if they are living or dead
The letters we write never reach their destination
and this war that separates us seems to go on forever

DREAMING OF LI PO

For someone who has died, our grief eventually ends
but when we separate from a friend, our sorrow never stops
I think of you exiled in a pestilent wilderness
I've heard no news of your condition
I think of you so deeply and so often
that must be why you come to me in dreams
How can you be here, I wonder
I thought you were snared in the Net of Consequences
The distance that separates us is so great
how will your spirit make its way back to your body
You journeyed here through green woods by day
and must return through the mountain passes at night
When I wake the moonlight lights up my room
I glimpse your ghostly face as if it were still here
Across the long night and deep waters you must go back
Be careful, old friend, don't let the water dragons get you!

THE GUEST

North and south of my hut the waters of spring flow
My only callers are the daily flocks of gulls
Without guests, no need to sweep petals from the path
But today I have opened my wicker gate for you
The market is far away, all I can offer is plain food
In my poor household, the wine is old and stale
But if you like, my elderly neighbor could join us
I'll call to him over the fence, he can help us drain our cups!

PASSING THE NIGHT AT HEADQUARTERS

Clear autumn, the wu-tung trees are cold beside the well
I am alone in River City, my candles are burning down
Through the long night, the sad sound of distant bugles
The moon crosses the sky, but I have no one to share it with
Endless war has cut off letters and news from friends
Travel is hard through the desolate frontier passes
For ten years I have endured trouble and hardship
and now I'm forced to roost on this lonely bough

NIGHT IN THE PAVILION

End of the year, yin and yang shorten the daylight
At the turning season, a night glazed with frost and snow
Fifth watch, the garrison's music makes a mournful sound
Over Three Gorges, the Milky Way spreads its luminous shadow
Because of the war, I hear families weeping in the countryside
Here and there a fisherman and woodcutter sing barbarian songs
Sleeping Dragon and the White Emperor have turned to yellow dust
No news from friends, how useless my sadness at the troubles of
      this world

NIGHT THOUGHTS WHILE TRAVELING

Near the bank where winds stir slender reeds
the solitary mast of my boat looms in the night
Stars hang low over the vast empty plain
and the moon wavers in the Great River's current
Poetry has not brought me fame or honor
Old age and illness have ended my career
What am I like in my aimless wanderings
but a gull drifting between heaven and earth

The Breeze from Malabar

from the ancient Sanskrit & Tamil

Spring arrives
with the song of the cuckoo
Bees swarm among flame trees
and a warm breeze from Malabar
fragrant as sandalwood
washes across the hearts of young lovers

Along the secret path
she quiets her jingling anklets
binding them in her skirt
But it's no use
The flowers in her hair
draw a swarm of blazing bees

Just over there
where willows overhang the riverbank
there's a chamber of green shade
with cool winds
and the music of waterbirds
Such a place, O handsome one,
what could it be for?
the village girl asks the traveler
her eyes on his

From across the great desert
her husband has returned
She meets him crying with joy
For his camel she brings palm leaves
and from its weary face
she wipes away the dust and sweat
with the hem of her dress

O sower of fields
how lovely is your new woman
that you desert this girl
whose beauty mirrors our village
with its lush lily fields
and sacred fires lighting the night
with tiny suns

First the blossoms of the jasmine
delight our eye
then its odor washes over us
We are moved by the poet's song
before we understand its meaning

Parrots have deserted its branches
Deer are gone who slept in its shade
Monkeys have fled who ate its fruit
The tree stands alone as the fire approaches

Little pearl, do not grieve
because waves have washed you ashore
Surely some king will walk by
Surely someone will set you in a crown

∾

The mother closes her arms
around her child
and the father of gentle words
embraces them both
In that small bed where they sleep
a sweetness greater than all the world

Pablo Neruda: Two Odes

ODE TO THE HUMMINGBIRD

To the hummingbird,
whirling
spark of water,
incandescent ember
of American fire,
flaming icon
of the jungle,
rainbow of celestial
precision:
to the hummingbird,
an arc,
a thread of gold,
a green blaze!

O
miniature
living flash
of lightning,
when you hover
in air
like a structure
of pollen,
like a feather
or ember,
I ask
what are you,
where did you come from?
Perhaps it was
in the blind ages
of the flood,

in the fertile mud
when the rose
crystallized within a fist of coal,
and metals
were forged
in secret chambers,
perhaps back then
a fragment
was chipped
from a wounded
dinosaur,
an atom
of gold,
the ultimate
cosmic scale,
a chip
of terrestrial fire,
and your iridescent
beauty
blazed
in a sudden sapphire.

You sleep
in a nut-shell,
you fit
in a tiny blossom,
little dart,
coin,
flicker of honey,
pollen-flash,
you are
so brave
even the black-plumed

falcon
doesn't frighten you:
whirling light
within light,
air within air,
you plunge
into the jewel box
of a trembling flower
unafraid of losing your head
in that nuptial honey.

You change from scarlet
to powdery gold,
from shimmering yellow
to a rare
ashen emerald,
to the orange-and-black velvet
of your radiant throat,
until you are
a blur,
a splinter of amber
from where you began,
supreme little one,
O miracle,
you blaze
from warm California
to the whistling
bitter wind of Patagonia.
You are
a seed of the sun,
plumed fire,
miniature
flag of wings,

petal of silenced people,
syllable
of our buried blood,
feathered crown
of our ancient
submerged
heart.

ODE TO THE NIGHT WASHERWOMAN

From the high garden
I watched the washerwoman.
It was night.
She washed, scrubbed,
shook out,
one second her hands
glistened in suds,
then
they fell into shadows.
By the light of a candle
she was in the night the only one
living,
the only one who lived:
that shaking out
in the suds,
her arms in the clothes,
the motion,
the tireless energy:
back and forth
the commotion,
falling and rising
with celestial precision,
back and forth
the immersed hands,
the hands, old hands
that wash in the night
until late in the night,
that wash
the clothes of strangers,
that remove in water
the prints of work,

the stain of bodies,
the memory of feet
that walked,
the worn-out shirts,
faded trousers,
she washes
and washes
in the night.

The nocturnal
washerwoman
sometimes
raised her head
and stars
glowed in her hair
because the darkness
bleared her head
and the night,
the sky
of night became
the hair
of the washerwoman
and her candle
a little
luminous star
that lit up her hands
which lifted
and shook the clothes,
rising
and
falling,
hoisting air,
water,

the slippery soap,
magnetic suds.

I couldn't hear,
couldn't hear
the rustle
of the clothes in her hands.
My eyes
in the night
gazed at her
alone
like a planet.
The nocturnal
washerwoman
glowed,
washing,
scrubbing
the clothes,
working
in the cold,
in the harshness,
washing in the nocturnal
silence of winter,
washing and washing
the poor
washerwoman.

PART FOUR

FIRE SEASON

Campfire

The light of my campfire goes only so far
into the darkness, into the shadowing trees
like shapes the shades might make
if they crossed over and came back among us.
I can see only so far into the night
the night I sat with my father before a campfire
in the Tehachapis. How ghostlike his image
appears to me now, how he seems almost a stranger,
and the boy sitting next to him, staring
into the flame, unable to make anything of it,
what do I make of him after all these years,
what could I tell him that he should know,
comforted as he is by the warmth of the fire
and the presence of his father sitting next to him
within the deep fatherless night surrounding them.

Fire Season

Lightning is the lord of everything
Heraclitus

SHAY CREEK

August. Clear morning.
A wisp of cloud above Burnside.
By noon it's grown to a thunderhead
drifting over the high country.
Then maybe a lightning flash
along the ridge, a burst
of thunder echoing downcanyon.
Soon there are strikes everywhere —
one bolt ignites a dead fir,
wind catches the blaze, spreads it,
fire moving faster than a man can run,
winds now whipping the flames,
limbs so full of pitch the trees explode
into a firestorm, the whole canyon on fire,
smoke drifting as far south as Mono.
Then come the fire teams,
hotshots with shovels and chain saws,
helicopters dangling water buckets,
bulldozers churning firebreaks,
a C-130 banking over the blaze
releasing chemical rain.
For days the forest burns.
Maybe weeks.
Sometimes they'll just let it burn
until it burns itself out.
Until the forest is all char and black ruins,

nothing left but scorched granite,
the skeletons of trees.
August in the high country.
Looking out from the cabin,
watching a cloud build.
The air dry and still.
Every August.
Looking up to the ridge
toward Burnside
where a thunderhead
is now massing.

THE AMADOR FIRE

The west slope is on fire,
the Gold Country is on fire —
juniper, pine, cedar — on fire —
smoke so thick you can look
directly into the red disk of the sun.
They've set a roadblock on 88,
a line of cars backed up half a mile,
Highway Patrol at the head,
lights flashing, ready to lead us
down the west slope to Amador.
Roll up the windows, here we go
into the smoke hole,
into the bardo of the burning world.
Along the roadside
hotshot crews in yellow jackets
armed with pulaskis and fire-rakes
climb out of the smoke and flames
having run for their lives.
They collapse on the shoulder,
faces blackened and streaked.
They'll make their stand here
along the edge of the highway,
cut down trees and bulldoze brush,
pray the fire won't crown,
won't cross over
and sweep east over the ridge
to Desolation and Eldorado
where the whole range might burn
as in apocalypse, the ending time,
no rapture, no paradise,

just flames and fire
eating fire, Amador
the summer of '04.

Rattlesnake

One spring morning driving up from Little Antelope Valley
over Monitor Pass and coming down into the Carson River
watershed and into Shay Creek country I come across a rattle-
snake lying stretched out in the middle of the road

for Kirby and Jake Wilkins

right *there* — a big mountain rattlesnake
its thick belly so bulged it wouldn't move,
so I park the Trooper on a turnout
and walk back with a hiking pole to prod
the snake off the road, but it won't budge
it's so full of something it had just swallowed,
a rabbit maybe, and the pavement's so warm
who wouldn't want to stretch out and nap
lulled and full in a kind of serpent happiness —
but this situation is serious, life or death,
there are among us those who wouldn't think twice
about running their car over this creature —
I don't want it to become another roadkill —
but no matter how much I prod and harass it,
the rattler won't move, so there's nothing to do
but grab it quickly by the tail and whip it
off the road, and it rolls over a few times,
alert now, and tries to coil into a striking position
but is so stuffed in the middle it can't manage it,
and now I prod it again and it makes a quick
side strike, mouth open, then snaps back, and begins
a slumberous lazy weave over the road's shoulder
and then down through rabbitbrush and boulders
toward the creek that flows into the East Fork
of the Carson where ten miles downriver
it will converge with Shay Creek that runs

past my cabin and where at night I listen
to the sound of water in the late spring
when snows are melting above Burnside
and the black bears are hunting for patches
of sunlight on the south side of the mountain
above the hot springs and where I'll soon
be sitting on my porch under an incense cedar
thinking about all of what in my life I did do,
and all of what, to my shame, I did not do.

The Woman in Black

She wears a black turtleneck sweater
black skirt with black fishnet stockings
and black boots
straight black hair to her shoulders
black eyeliner and crimson lipstick
and she is drinking a cappuccino in the Caffe Trieste
Corelli streaming from a speaker
and if you're eighteen
and in North Beach for the first time
and it's 1961 and you've fled from your little town
and you think you might be a poet
would you not yearn for the woman in black
who lights a Gauloise and gazes off somewhere
does not notice the young man or feel his ardor
does not know that fifty years later
he will put her — *here* — in this poem

Let Me Tell You

Ellen's geese attacked me
every time I came to visit
they'd see me walk up
and the assault was on
they'd rush *hissing*
long necks erect
beaks that could grip
like a pair of pliers
and twist an inch of skin
off the arm you raised
to ward them off
and then with their wings
the edge of their wings
they'd slam you
with the force of a two-by-four
and this happened
every time I came
they never got used to me
and I couldn't
make friends with them
I don't know what
it was about me
maybe Ellen
was telling them stories
behind my back
telling them what
a jerk
I could be
(and forty years later
everyone agrees
I still can be)

and you ask me
how'd you come by
that scar on your arm
well let me
tell you

Foundation Work: Shay Creek

for Clem Starck

All summer that first year working under
the cabin where some idiot years before
had built a post-and-pier foundation
on six-foot centers. Didn't he know
this is earthquake country, that Shay Creek
sits on a fault where two plates collide,
one grinding under the other, uplifting
a mountain range four hundred miles long
and still rising. So all summer I shored up
the foundation, put in new four-by-four posts
three feet on center, built cross-braces
and plywood shear walls — all summer
down there, in the dead air, handkerchief
tied over my face, like a bandit, sweating,
breathing hantavirus, bent over, back
aching, cracking my head on floor joists —
and the thing of it all — no one
would notice, would ever *see* the work,
and soon enough I wouldn't think of it,
sitting on the porch in the afternoons,
light slanting through the pines, maybe
drinking a little wine, reading poems,
attending quietly to someone's words,
not thinking about what holds them
together, how the sounds cohere,
unaware of the foundation under it all,
the hidden labor, the bedrock of song.

The Cave

Who wants to be the first to go
into the cave behind the cabin
in the Tehachapis where three boys
three brothers try to work out
the order of entrance because all
are a little afraid of what
for-god's-sake might be in there —
pit vipers spiders vampire bats
maybe a waking bear — so — *you*
go first — no you — no you go —
until one does go crawling on all fours
into the darkness into the dank
cold air that smells of something
not human not even animal
something old and alien something
that enters the boy as he crawls out
into the night and finds his brothers
gone his parents many years dead
while in the great cave over him
stars shimmer like bees in a hive
as he traces in the zodiac
the shape of a beast
opening its maw as if alive

Early in the Twenty-First Century

In Cavtat on the Dalmatian coast
about ten miles south of Dubrovnik
there's an abandoned house, a villa actually,
owned by Serbs who dare not come back
into Croatia, and it isn't clear to anyone
what will become of this place
settling into ruin, a few windows broken,
the garden gone wild where one day
I found a tortoise wandering the grounds —
and where are those Serbs who lived here
I wondered, who were once neighbors
in this neighborhood, before the old hatreds
kindled — Orthodox vs. Catholic
vs. Muslim vs. Jew — one atrocity avenged
by another, until it all went up in flames —
civility, tolerance, trust, goodwill —
though today you wouldn't know it,
the folk hereabouts are friendly, people
are laughing in the cafés, there's fine wine,
boats leave every hour for the scenic cruise
to Dubrovnik, there's ice cream, swimming,
and summer tourists, and you wouldn't know
anything had happened in this little village
other than that empty villa, slowly collapsing,
with its ancient tortoise plodding aimlessly
in a garden choking with weeds.

Night Psalms

IN THE TERROR TIME

so many miracles under the sky

no lie

the grape bears witness
crushed into wine

drink up

you can die
before you die

∾

lord
of tender mercies

listen

with machetes
they're butchering babies

what
should we trust?

tell again

your infinite love
for us

∾

rain
on shed tin roof

orchestra
of dead names

∾

on the other side
of the broken window

a broken world

when the daughter dies
her father cries

everything in season
for no clear reason

∾

lord
reveal the *meaning*

of the child's body
searched for

by dogs

∾

star

blown apart
light-years ago

any night its absence

reaching us

~

lord

maker of milk and nectar
venom and dew

maker of hummingbird
and its needle

of morning glory
fired with sapphire

maker of leaf
and leaf-shaped adder's head

for you these incantations
incarnations

for you
the singing and murdering

~

lord
must the child thank you

for the day
when with an axe

they broke through the door
of joy

broke into her little room
of song

∾

this the shade under the persimmon tree
these the falling suns

O crow among branches
whetting its beak

choosing the ripest one

∾

down what road
toward what country

following the white ox

into the sun

Becoming Human

From bits of jawbone, pelvis, a femur,
anthropologists reconstruct the skeleton
of *Homo habilis*, a primate who looks part ape,
part human, earliest ancestor of *Homo sapiens*.
We know this creature used crude stone tools
and lived in small groups, a hunter-gatherer
on the African savanna two million years ago.
But we don't know whether they could speak,
whether they had a language beyond gutturals
or grunts. We know they could walk upright,
but we know nothing of those nights
when they slept together — did they hold
and comfort each other? What did they make
of the stars crossing over? And at dawn
when the sun rose, did they catch their breath?
Were they able to laugh and weep, could they
imagine, *envision*, their own unthinkable,
personal death?

On Green Dolphin Street

in memory of Robert McNamara Burrows

The room was dark, all the curtains closed
as my cousin paced from one wall to another,
sweating, talking, an addict trying to kick
his habit cold turkey. I was there to be
with him, help ease him through his hard time.
We talked mostly about jazz; he was a drummer,
and we both had a wild love for the music,
so we talked as he paced — Your favorite group?
Miles with Coltrane and Bill Evans —
Your favorite song? "On Green Dolphin Street" —
And this went on — Art Pepper, Horace Silver, Monk,
as Robert walked back and forth, drumming in his mind
to an old blues that he began humming — *Down
on the killing floor* — which is where they found him
a year later, an OD — Robert — my cousin, the oldest
of our clan's children, a good man and musician,
a drummer who could keep a perfect tempo,
but who loved to get up on the beat, between
the 2 and 4, the way Miles liked it, a beat
within the beat, a tiny hitch in time like
a caught breath, a little kick urging the soloist
to step forth, open up, and wail.

Passage

*Guidavaci una voce che cantava
di là; e noi, attenti pur a lei,
venimmo fuor là ove si montava.*

Purgatorio XXVII, 55–57

Mid-September, 5:00 a.m., still night outside,
I hear the garbage truck grinding down my street.
I've been thinking of a poet who is dying in New York,
how these days she reads her beloved Dante,
perhaps looking for something to frame
what is happening to her.
And whom, I wonder, do I turn to?
Whom in this century do I read
as if my life depended upon it?
The garbage truck stops at my driveway.
Two men are arguing, or laughing,
I can't tell,
as they empty the can and drop it onto the street.
There are some who believe the poem can be a guide,
a Virgil, can be a window into a way of being.
Do I believe this? Does anyone believe this anymore?
My dying friend is reading a poem that speaks of love
as a fire, as a wall of flame the body must pass through.
The truck continues down the block.
Lights are coming on in the houses.
It's almost day. People are getting ready for work.
TVs are on. Radios are on.
I can hear more garbage being emptied
and then a can clanging onto concrete.
I'm thinking of my dying friend,
of Dante who says our life is a passage,

how a voice sings beyond the flame,
guiding us, how we must pass through the fire
if we are to begin the ascent.

PART FIVE

CONVERGENCE

Convergence

Mystery train comin', comin' down the track
Mystery train comin', won't be comin' back

Coming toward us down the track was a tramp
so Richard stepped off the rail and said *Watch this*
and dropped his cigarette and after we passed the guy
Richard stopped and we looked back and sure enough
he was bending over and picking up the butt
and he took a long drag I could almost taste with him
the sweet tobacco and the hit of nicotine and Richard
laughed and punched my arm and I laughed because
we were both fourteen and stupid and walking home
from school this was in Santa Fe Springs on a train track
through cow pastures and dairy farms and it was
early spring and California everywhere was green
and Vietnam was nowhere in our world and neither
of us knew that not too far ahead down another
kind of track Richard would find himself in a green jungle
that blazed like fire that at times caught fire where one day
he too would stop to take a hit his hand rising to his mouth
as if in surprise as if in a gesture to shut back speech as if
to say nothing could be said about the streak of silver
that flashed down the track and he took the hit tasting it
deep in his lungs as his friends turned to look back and saw him
in slow motion and wonder sag to his knees where the rails
finally converged and disappeared with his life

Against Surrealism

I

I saw once in Vietnam along the side of a road a boy sleeping
sprawled across the back of a water buffalo as big as a car a
buffalo standing in a rice paddy and itself slumbering its head
with up-curved horns swaying slowly and in the shade under
it an egret holding in the tip of its beak a frog as green as the
emerald shoots of rice planted by those women stooped over
and up to their knees in mud the color of the buffalo on whose
great wide shoulders the boy woke and turned to me a child's
Buddha-like smile of inscrutable mystery

2

From a restaurant terrace on the island of Symi I look out over
fields of poppies and see working its way down the mountain
a burro being led by an old Greek the beast rocking from side
to side with what appear from this distance to be bundles of
flowers strapped to its back and I return to the plate before me
continue to disassemble with a fork the skeleton of a sculpin
when down the cobbled street comes the burro and as it passes
under me I see lashed to its back the slaughtered flayed-out
carcasses of goats and the old Greek looks up whistling a
dirge I heard played on a lyra in the church courtyard on Good
Friday when the village widows dressed in black let down
their hair whipping it keening and flailing over the laid-out
wooden corpse of a bearded young man the one they say was an
incarnate god who walked among us for a time

3

Pacific Avenue — Del Mar Theatre, Palace Art, Bookshop Santa Cruz — strolling on a Saturday afternoon in spring, the first bright day after weeks of rain and fog. You pass a booth selling coffee and chai, a whiff of ganja in the air, and stop before a long window with its beach scene — mannequins, torsos in swimsuits, an assemblage of sandals, the window shimmering in light, the way memory shimmers, shimmering into a temple in Varanasi with sandals piled outside, the Ganges flowing past, a corpse struggling in the current, on the bank a buzzard clacking its tongue, there's a white marble palace, burning ghats, spirits unfleshed, and now voices singing down Pacific Avenue, down this long shimmering pane of glass wavering your reflection and the image of a woman behind you, a street performer, juggling the heads of dolls, at her feet a hat filling with coins.

Passing Through: A Stroll
at the End of the Twentieth Century

Walking down Ocean View, I'm pushing Charis in a wheelchair and Rachel is pointing out all the neighborhood flowers. Santa Cruz, autumn 1997. Clear, warm days for weeks with no morning fog. They say it's El Niño. They say it's going to be the wettest winter of the century. A cat pads out to the sidewalk to greet Charis. They're old friends. The cat leaps onto Charis's lap, and she strokes it. Rachel is singing something incomprehensible under her breath. Somewhere above us the *Mir* is also making sounds, a disaster waiting to happen according to NASA's computers. The cat leaps off Charis, and we continue our stroll. South of here, off the coast of Carmel, there's an oil spill, containment forthcoming says the news, but not in time for hundreds of seabirds tarred with oil to wash ashore. We pass a row of ornate Victorians, "painted ladies," built in the last century. Last year one owner had a helicopter hover and lower a thirty-foot palm into a hole. He didn't want to wait thirty years. Instant landscape. And a palm tree where no palm tree should be. Ah, California. Some say *you* are the future. My guess is China. Or Bosnia. Rachel accuses me of gloom and doom. *Think good thoughts*, she says. I think of our passing century. Who could have known in the fin-de-siècle world what the following years would bring. Somme. Auschwitz-Birkenau. Hiroshima. The list is endless. My Lai. Rwanda. Killing fields. Famines. My own, and everyone's, complicity. Yes, I know what Adorno said. *And yet...and yet...* is what Issa said. *Think good thoughts*, Rachel says. I will. I do. I think I love this little walk, this stroll, this moment we have on a planet bathed in the light of a minor star on the outer arm of a galaxy in a universe hurtling apart. Charis hasn't many years left. And I'm right behind her. Soon all this will be only someone's memory, and then that too will be gone. But how sweet to be here, in this moment. We reach the park and look out over the bluff toward the Boardwalk with its Ferris wheel and Big Dipper, to the bay, which is calm, and beyond to the immense Pacific where gray whales are making their passage from Alaska to Baja. We pause in our passage, our little walk from here to there, from then to now, and now turn around, beginning the slow stroll back.

Standing Before Dylan's Grave in Laugharne
with John Logan, Summer 1976

We were both drunk having staggered out of the pub
after drinking with some old local who said he knew Dylan
and was using this to cadge drinks from us and told story
after story of high jinks and low jinks each one more
outrageous than the last and they were good stories
and we were happy to keep them coming and keep
the ale flowing caught up in the Welsh gift for gab
and then there we were standing before Dylan's
little white cross made of wood a shameful thing
the villagers said of Caitlin too broke or drunk
to penny-up for marble both of us standing there
lost in our thoughts my own of my mother reading
aloud from his poems Dylan was my first love as a poet
and you never get over that one but I don't want to wallow
in nostalgia I want a poem that brims with anger and rage
like the rage Dylan raised against the death
of his father and against his own death for we all know
all elegies are self-elegies so a rage against cheap poems
and easy sentiments an anger to burn away the frivolous
posing and posturing of poems my own among them
and most of all a rage against the Great Leveler
the Butcher Boy an anger against the inescapable
inexorable train-wreck day when the Lord of the Dead
took Dylan away then took John away and one day
will open my door and all my five and country senses
will finally see whether Dylan's vision was a true vision
and whether or not Death shall have no dominion

Sitting on a Bench in the Plaza of Mendoza
Watching the Skeletons

(Lophophora williamsii)

Some of them talking
to themselves
others pushing strollers with children
their little skulls with living eyes
unaware
of the coming disaster
the families seem happy
caught in the in-between time
and passing time
under the pepper trees
passing away the hours
lulled by the moment
of being alive
their skeletons fleshed out
under the meat-eating sun

Some kids are laughing
at a squirrel
its skeleton
jangling in the limbs
of a tree
as a kid's hand holds out
a nut
which the squirrel takes
in its mouth
sits up
and with delicate paws
turns the nut over and over
as the kids laugh

hak hak hak
their little skeletons
rattling with glee

A policewoman in shorts
and helmet
rides a bike
a pistol strapped to her hip bone
the bike like the skeleton
of some future creature
both skeletons
wheeling through time
mocking gravity
the pull to earth
where it all ends
in the end

A fortune-teller
on a bench
her skull
wrapped in a bandanna
clutches in her hands
the upturned hand
of a young woman
who is weeping
the fortune-teller's jaws
opening and closing
make human sounds
one skeleton
talking to another

Canis latrans lestes

And then Coyote walked into the world where the first
humans were sitting in the cold and Coyote showed them how
to build a fire where they could warm themselves and then
Coyote took off his hat and had the people look into it and
what they saw were themselves looking into a hat

There's a big coyote on the path below the cabin,
howling and yipping, I think he's calling to Rose,
my golden retriever, I think he wants to mate with her,
or maybe kill her, and Rose, inside the cabin, alert,
is also making sounds, ones I've never heard before,
I don't know whether she's terrified or she's interested,
so I step outside and call to the coyote, invite him
to come on over, let me introduce you to her,
but he's no fool, he knows all humans are crazy
and know nothing of how life in the wilderness
finds a way to survive, so when I walk outside
he takes off, trotting, lifting his paws, you could
call it strutting, the haughty son-of-a-bitch, not even
looking back at me, or at Rose, who might have just
missed the love of her life, or the loss of her life,
and we spend the next few moments in our own
strange selves on this side of a mountain somewhere
in the twenty-first century, the Age of Termination,
where only the cunning will survive,
like those coyotes, wandering in the last, desolate cities.

Without Apollo, without Duino

Her mother couldn't stop her, her friends couldn't stop her, no one could stop her from taking her life. A student at the college. Quiet in class, diligent, all her essays turned in on time, except the last one, unfinished, a rough draft, the thesis just an insight — *Everything's broken.* She had been reading Rilke, about looking at the broken torso of Apollo and imagining a face with eyes ripening like fruit. Like Rilke, she had discovered there's nowhere, no place where you cannot be found. Her friends tell me she was hearing voices near the end. Angelic? Demonic? What did they say, these voices, whispering what story against which she had no defense, no way to not listen? *Everything is far and long gone by* Rilke wrote in his early, saccharine style. Then he heard voices. Standing in a storm before the gates of Castle Duino, he heard the songs of Angelic Orders, voices that could annihilate his life, and would have, had he not found his own voice as a way of singing back into the voiceless, broken world.

Tiresias on Cold Mountain

How dreadful knowledge of the truth can be
When there's no help in truth

Sophocles

Yet I ask you to look at the wooden puppets
Worn out by their moment of play on the stage

Han-shan

Tiresias retires to a hut in the mountains above Thebes.
He's dismissed the boy who would describe for him
the flight of birds. No more prophesying, no more
reaching inside a slaughtered beast to read the future.
A simple stone hut. There's not much time left.
He knows how the gods reach into our flesh
and scatter our lives across the years.
He must prepare himself for what's coming.
He's afraid. He remembers how adamant he'd been
with Oedipus. How accurate. Oedipus who persisted
in discovery, who walked into exile, ravaged and blind,
tapping with a cane, fulfilling the riddle. Tiresias knows
the formula: *Attention. Discipline. Vision.*
He must prepare. His heart has grown old and soft.
He doesn't know how he will act, what he will do
when Apollo comes down, when the Wolf God
is upon him.

The Bodhisattva in Jane Austen

Our heroine rides a horse next to the lord
of the manor who has yet to discover he is
in love with her. Devon. Early summer.
They ride across fields and pass a millpond,
hardly notice the boy fishing on its bank.
He is to them absolutely nothing as they
ride past into their intricate plot. The boy
stays. He has no home, for Austen has
imagined him none. He stares into the water,
the clouds crossing over. He has no other
story, no other life but this one, the one
between the covers of a book, this one
moment in which to be, where he forever
is.

If You're Travelin' in the North Country Fair

Kabul, the Apsara Hotel, dirt cheap, a dormitory on the second floor full of travelers, an oil stove leaking smoke, February 1975, the coldest winter of my life. Over in a corner, a French girl strums her guitar. She's in love with Dylan. The men in the room are in love with Morphine. Two Italians sit on the bed next to my cot. The one with long black hair and black beard, shining eyes, has rolled up his sleeve. Most of that morning I had wandered the streets, stunned by the cold sweeping down from the steppes. I was looking for the black market and Jalad, the six-fingered money-changer. I believed at that time that if I could just get to a certain place, I would be okay. That the journey alone might redeem me. A week before, traveling through the Hindu Kush and over Khyber Pass with its tribal men holding ancient, handcrafted rifles, I heard rumors of a far-off valley, a hidden kingdom somewhere out past Swat, almost to the Karakorams — no roads into it, Westerners forbidden. It was important to me that it be secluded — that to get to it I would have to leave everything of my old life behind. What *was it* I so yearned to find? There was no chance of my making that journey. I had other plans — to move overland through Kandahar, Herat, Tabriz, and on to Athens by spring where Rachel would join me. We didn't know it, but we were going to live in a small village on the island of Kárpathos. We were going to live together for the last time. Sitting on my cot in the Apsara, I watch the bearded one fall back into his paradise, the needle still in his arm. His friend is arguing with a Tajik boy about a pair of hand-tooled boots that are too small. The French girl begins singing another Dylan song. I sit on the edge of my cot, hands jammed into my jacket, a snowstorm swirling outside, a savage, alien winter blazing within me.

In the Shadow of Trees

in memory of my grandfather,
Robert McNamara

Highland Park in the late Forties, sycamores and elms in the arroyo, a few pepper trees on Branch Street. Five years old, I'm standing under a fig tree with my grandfather. He snaps a fig from a branch. Milk oozes from the stem. With two thumbs he splits open the fruit, its flesh full of seeds, looking like specks of stars as if there had been a galaxy within. Years after he died, I visited Inishmore off the coast of Galway, making the journey for him, for our McNamara blood. I was surprised how there were no trees on the island — just rock, a blasting sea, fields with stone walls, black cliffs. When Ellen and I moved to Santa Cruz, the first thing I did was plant trees — a fig tree in memory of my grandfather, and a lemon tree to grow up with little Sam. Each year the fig tree bore two crops, and it was a race between Sam and the lemon as to who was growing faster. Then came the afternoon when Ellen and Sam were burying a pet canary. Sam had a shovel and was digging a hole next to the fig tree. I walked over, upset that he was digging it too close to the roots — *Pay attention to what you're doing,* I said. Sam, ten years old, looked up, his face confused with betrayal and grief. Ellen stood there, holding the bird in a washcloth, its wire-like feet clutching nothing, the tiny beak slightly open. Under the February clouds the day poured down over our little group. Sam rested his foot on the shovel, looking down into the grave he had dug. Ellen kneeled and placed the bird into the earth, as I stood there, wordless and ashamed, under the fig tree and within the memory of an old man whose words once were a comfort and a hope for me.

Monastery, Andalucía, End of the Twentieth Century

The monastery is a three-hour walk from Cazorla, through olive groves, vineyards, a pine forest. Only one monk lives here now — Brother Antoñio, eighty years old. From the barred window of his cell I can see the cliffs of the Sierra de Segura. A knotted-rope scourge hangs on a wall — no longer used, Antoñio informs me. Once, many monks lived in this monastery, but in the Civil War in this part of Andalucía the locals sided with the Loyalists, so they sacked the place. A lot of blood in these mountains. Lorca walked here. And Machado. In nearby Úbeda, a church keeps the preserved arm of Saint John of the Cross. Descending a stairway, Antoñio guides me past the brothers' cells, until we reach the bottom — a chapel hewn out of the stone of the cliff, an altar flickering with candles, icons, an agonized Christ on his cross, remnants of a medieval world when all across Europe great cathedrals were rising into the vault of heaven. There is one more room Antoñio wants to show me, under the chapel, an ossuary, a catacomb of skulls and bones. Antoñio looks fondly at his brothers, gently touching the forehead of a skull that grimaces back at him. Maybe a friend, someone he once knew. *Vengo aquí frecuentemente*, he tells me. He seems a kind, gentle man. Each morning he works in his garden — tomatoes, bean plants on poles, a small vineyard. He cures olives, tends a few hives, gathering the white honey of rosemary. Upstairs in his small kitchen he fills a goblet with wine, offers it to me, then pours one for himself. We drink in silence. When I prepare to leave, he thanks me for my visit. *Solo pocos vienen ahora.* On my walk back to Cazorla, I gaze up at the cliffs of the Sierra de Segura where raptors can sometimes be seen rising and wheeling in invisible thermals.

La Doncella of Llullaillaco

God lives in the sun, god becomes
a condor rising over the Andes —
where is my mother, my father,
I have been left here, on this
platform on the peak of Llullaillaco —
I will be the sacrifice, I will be
food for the god, for the one
whose hands are talons, the plumed god
who will pick my bones clean
that he might be appeased, that the rains
might come, for our crops had failed —
my people chose me, a fourteen-year-old girl,
and then a little boy, and a younger girl,
for a year they kept us apart from the rest,
fed us, nursed and blessed us, I became
an *accla*, I would be the gift,
the sacrifice our people must make —
I did not hate what would happen to me
but I was afraid. They said I would become
part of the god, I would fly into the sun,
my blood would come down as rain,
I would be born again, I would live beyond the sky —
so we began the long walk, with elders and priests,
for six months, through arroyos, playas, salt flats,
to the puna of Atacama below the volcano —
each step took me closer to what I would become,
I tried to imagine what it would be like
to be up there in air so fine a fire will not catch,
would I feel pain, would the god
be quick, would I be riven in flames —
the last days they gave us *coca* to chew,

chicha to drink, and then we began the ascent —
the girl could keep nothing down,
and the boy, that poor boy, could not breathe,
could not make the climb, he died below
and they wrapped him with ropes, carried him
on their back, laid him beside me, silent,
then left us on our platform for the god to come —
like stones we were, and the deep night
came down over us, the cold entered us,
the stars a thousand eyes of the night god —
and with dawn the sun rose, the girl
had died in the night, the sun touched
all the peaks of the cordillera, blazing in light,
and my heart caught fire, I saw all the lives
I might have lived, I saw my mother, my father,
I saw a husband with my child, I saw what
life I might have been given, had I been free,
when the sun god in a spear of light
took me.

The End of Romanticism

San Francisco State, 1963

in memory of Professor Julian

These late spring days feel like summer, cherries and apricots already in the markets. I know some of you are weary of Blake and "Intimations of Immortality." But before we end the term, I want to say a few words about someone not on your reading list: Charles Lamb. He was born in London's Inner Court, grew up with taverns and bookstores as his backyard. A man of keen intelligence, among the first to recognize the worth of Coleridge and Wordsworth. He wrote a curious prose:

> *Sun, and sky, and breeze, and solitary walks, and summer holidays, and the greenness of fields, and the delicious juices of meats and fishes, and society, and the cheerful glass, and candlelight, and fireside conversations, and innocent vanities, and jests, and* irony itself — *do these things go out with life?*

But there is something else about his life I want you to know. In a letter to Coleridge, he writes — *God has preserved to me my senses... With me the "former things are passed away," and I have something more to do than to feel.* He's speaking of a horror that took place when he was twenty-two years old, about the age of some of you. His sister, Mary, had what we would call a psychotic breakdown. Their word for it was *lunacy*. Lamb was there to witness it. He was unable to restrain Mary from plunging a knife into their mother's heart. Imagine for a moment recollecting that in tranquillity. Mary was ruled insane, and confined to Bedlam, a hospital as bad as a prison. After a stay, she was released into

Lamb's care. For the rest of his life he looked after her. Together they wrote *Tales from Shakespeare*. And everyone who visited their household was charmed by Mary's kindness and grace. She fussed over the young Keats, and could even make the dour Mister Wordsworth stop talking and smile. But her illness ran deep — from time to time it would begin to surface, and she had to be returned to the madhouse. When the symptoms passed, she was freed again into Lamb's care. Mary and Lamb became able to recognize the stages of her illness, could see when it was beginning to take over, and they knew she had no defense. All semester we've been discussing Romanticism, the Sublime, the articulation of Personal Emotion and the power of Imagination. Now imagine this. Holding each other, carrying the restraining straps with them, Mary and Lamb, sobbing, walked the long road back to Bedlam.

PART SIX

ALL WE HAVE OF PARADISE

Flowers

And my house, Rafael, remember?
And you, Federico, under the earth,
do you remember my house of flowers?

Pablo Neruda

Why all the flowers in your house? my visitor asks —
yellow tulips on the kitchen windowsill,
sunflowers in a tall glass vase on the table,
Peruvian lilies, oxeye daisies, flaming nasturtiums.
I tell him winter is coming, the long nights are coming.
I tell him flowers are the candles of my spirit,
they are a balance between stars and sorrow.
Oh, he says, *I thought someone might've died.*
Someone *has* died, I say, all my friends are dying.
I, too, can see the tunnel up ahead, and I don't think
there's light at the end of it. Therefore in this world
I place flowers throughout my house: they light up
my rooms, they are a kind of quiet burning,
and their evanescence makes me attend to what
is important in my life, among other things,
for example, these flowers.

Reading Horace the Summer of My Sixty-Eighth Year

Write in your book as profit every new day
Quintus Horatius Flaccus

On the hillside that steps down to the cabin
where I have seen my self rise out of myself
and walk into the warm resinous summer air,
walk away from the cabin, climb the hillside
up past the boulders, deer trails, the charred
limbs of a cedar struck by lightning years ago,
heart laboring, deep breaths, wondering if maybe
it will happen today, maybe today walking
into my sixty-eighth year I will see once more
what is there before me — the everyday rapture
of what *is*.

Translating Neruda the Year My Father Was Dying

I translated thirty odes of Pablo Neruda,
my Spanish so poor, so broken and tawdry,
I had to check each word in the dictionary.
Forgive me, Pablo, but my father was dying.
I needed something — *anything* — to hold to.
I know you have many translators,
but none of them, and this I swear to you,
none of them, *compadre*, lived in your poems
the way I lived, holding on to the little artichoke,
a pair of socks, the smell of firewood at night.

Hunting Chanterelles,
Majors Creek, Santa Cruz Mountains

Crawled
over leaf fall and duff
through ferns and nightshade
a week after the first rains
on all fours crawled
like an animal
down in the undergrowth
among sedge and adder's-tongue
down there
in the other world
no yesterday no tomorrow
no Buddha no sorrow

Hovering

for Tom Marshall

Tom and I are walking Last Chance Road
down from the mountain where we had been
hunting mushrooms under a stand of coast oaks,
walking down and looking out to the Pacific
shimmering in the late fall sun, the light
on the surface like glittering flakes of mica,
when we see a white-tailed kite hovering
in the air, hovering over a green pasture,
hovering over the day, over the two of us,
our very lives hovering as well, there
on the California coast, in the fall, in the sun,
on our way home, with a sack of chanterelles,
with our love for this world, with so much time,
and so little time — all of it — hovering —
and hovering still.

Some Glad Mornings

And how, you ask, do I now abide my days.
Some days I sit on my porch, like old folk do,
sometimes with a book and a cup of coffee,
other times looking intently at what is before me,
or letting the memories come, the sweet ones,
and the bitter, the tonic, and now I am tossing
some almonds for those two crows who come
and wait each morning, looking at me as if
I might be someone worth knowing, certainly
worth waiting for what I give them; and what
do they give me — Delight? Joy? — Oh yes,
and a frame for this moment in which to be,
thankful for their presence — their sleek
crow clarity and the bright *caws*
of their coal-black company.

Blast

Driving up Poor Boy Road in four-wheel drive —
steep grade, rocks and ruts, my old Trooper doing
what it was made to do — I reach a washout,
get out, and walk a mile or so into the forest,
hear a sound, something I can't identify, and come
to a meadow, maybe two or three acres, at its center
a vernal pool, will be bone dry come summer,
but now, sitting in its middle, about two feet deep,
a black bear, splashing the water around him,
having fun, enjoying the day, and I don't care
what they say about giving animals human feelings,
call it projection, magical thinking, whatever, this bear —
this big cinnamon-colored bear — is having a blast!

Whiteout

First big storm of the year. Snow level
dropping to two thousand feet. Blizzards
on the passes. Icy roads. Whiteouts.
This morning I can hear the distant *frump*
of dynamite tearing avalanches from cliffs
above the Spur. No one's going anywhere
in the Sierra today. Nothing to do but shove
a chunk of wood into the stove, put on
some Brahms, and watch snow sift down
in a silence of white ash. Nothing to do
but take a book from the shelf, open to Tu Fu,
and trace his words like animal tracks scrawling
across the white page where a white crane rises
out of the snow's white pavilion.

Poem in the Sung Manner

in memory of Mort Marcus

Mort — remember how we used to tangle
over poetry, how I held the T'ang dynasty
superior to your favorite, the Sung, how we'd
sit in my little shed, drinking, swapping stories,
the talk flowing between us, all those words
like all those years we shared, our friendship
going deeper as we grew older — old friend,
no one knows how much I miss you —
your quick laughter, your wit and candor —
I would give anything to be with you again.
Now I sit alone in my shed thinking of you,
reading Sung poems from a thousand years ago
and come to the one by Mei Yao-ch'en
the night he's sharing the last of his wine
with his old friend who will be leaving
in the morning on a journey from which
he will not return.

Flashback: First Song

One day,
hiking the high trail out of Wolf Creek,
a door opened — and I entered Ruth's farm
where my grandmother stood looking out
to the horses near the pond, the willows,
the porch with its trellis heavy with wisteria,
and for the first time
I glimpsed a luminous world
within our world. Then the door closed,
and I was back in the Sierra, among lupine,
juniper, granite, hiking the high trail,
holding within me the song of memory,
the horses standing quiet and huge,
the long slow breathing of wisteria,
a morning where everything was singing,
and where a small boy, alone in his life,
looked into the jewel at the center of time.

Gone

One of my chores as a boy was to take out
the trash and empty it in our backyard burner.
I loved lighting the match, its quick-blue plume
setting the paper on fire, the yellow flames,
white smoke rising into our orange tree.
This was in a small California town surrounded
with orange groves all the way to the sea
where on spring nights their odor filled my life.
No backyards have trash burners now
and all the orange groves have disappeared,
replaced with housing tracts, malls, freeways.
What's gone is gone, my father used to say,
as if saying this somehow lessened the loss.
My father is gone, and my mother, and words
don't make their loss easier, though words are all
I have to make something out of what has gone
as I look back at that boy standing in his yard,
burning the trash, not knowing the groves
around him would soon be uprooted, bulldozed
into pyres, and set on fire, lighting up in my mind
those gone California nights of another time.

Riven

On my way back to London I have to wait for a train
in Carmarthen, so I enter a pub, some locals at the bar,
everyone in good cheer, holding pints, when one of them
drops to the floor like he's been axed, his arms and legs
thrashing, eyes rolled back in his head. His friends
don't appear surprised, a few bend down, hold him,
in a moment it's over, and they help him to a chair,
and the talk resumes. I stand there gripping a pint
of bitter, recalling the Laugharne churchyard
where I stood before the grave of the Welsh singer,
listening in memory to my mother reading his poetry,
and now thinking of her and her last days, helpless
and dying, no one to hold her, to raise her up,
no poetry, her memory flailing and thrashing
within me.

Khe Sanh, Revisited

Imagine
a grenade in the hand of a ten-year-old boy,
holding it out to you, the pin still in it,
holding it out as if he wanted to give it to you,
as if you needed to hold it to understand what
happened in Khe Sanh before this boy was born,
in a war that killed his grandfather, grandmother.
Here, take the grenade, he seems to say. He wants you
to buy it, something from the USA. You reach out
your hand, there's so much you've never held.
The boy is smiling. All around is farmland,
coffee fields, paths with signs warning *UXO*.
Take the grenade, hold it in your hand, imagine
what happened to the man who once held it.
Imagine being sent to a country on the other side
of the world — to do what, and for whose reason.
Imagine putting the grenade inside a poem,
clenched there, with your memories and desires,
those bright mornings shining ahead, each day
a slow unfolding of the mystery, and the poem
imagining it all, a new world about to begin.
And now, imagine, pulling the pin.

The Poet King

And so we come at last
to the banks of the Perfume River
where Tu Duc,
Poet King of the Nguyen Dynasty,
wanted to make on earth
his earthly paradise.
Here are his gardens and pavilions.
Here is the Pleasure Dome
where he held court —
where courtiers could speak
only in poetry.
Over there is the Pool of Contemplation
where koi swirl like brushstrokes
writing invisible poems in water.
Can you imagine Tu Duc
sitting in his dragon robe
writing immortal poems?
Can you imagine a king
who wanted to show us
how a poet might rule —
feasts that went on for weeks,
fifty-course meals,
tea brewed from the dew
of a thousand lotus blossoms —
and rhyming contests,
laws of the kingdom
composed as poems.
That was his world.
And this is the King's Arena
where Tu Duc watched
the royal elephant

crush a Bengal tiger —
the great cat tied to a stake.
Can you picture Tu Duc
with his one hundred wives,
his village of concubines,
the three thousand workmen
he worked to death
building his mausoleum?
And here it is
with its Hall of the King
where a carved jade dragon
rises over his tomb.
Imagine Tu Duc
imagining in a poem
the true Dragon streaming in fire
across the River of Heaven.
Imagine poetry as a country
ruled by Tu Duc
who near the banks of the Perfume River
wanted to turn our world
into his vision
of paradise.

Carrying the Pig

Above Sa Pa two men are carrying
a 200-pound pig hanging upside down,
stretched out, its feet tied to a thick
bamboo pole hefted on the shoulders
of the men who are struggling to hold
the pig off the ground, it's so heavy
and the path so muddy, the pig
is squealing, bawling, as if being
murdered, as it will be, soon enough,
first the men have to make it all the way
to Cat Cat, the village below,
a long walk on a steep,
slippery path, and the villagers of Sa Pa
have come out to see how this
is going to work — some
offering advice, others making bets,
it's a festive mood and these hill people
work so hard all day long they
cherish this moment, except
those two poor guys struggling
with the pig, when the man in back
does slip and down goes the pig
into the mud and now it's really howling
and the man is having a hard time
getting back on his feet and the pig
is flinging mud everywhere so the man
in front is getting splattered while the crowd
laughs for tonight there will be a festival
and feast in the village below — the one finally
makes it to his feet and he and the pig
and the other man disappear down the path,

and now others walk past carrying baskets,
holding chickens with their feet tied together,
and down the path they go as night comes on
and fireworks begin going off far below —
a skyrocket streaks up in the dark
and bursts into an emerald shriek
like the embodied, almost human cry
of a pig being slaughtered in the sky.

One Morning near the Lake of the Returned Sword

You walk along the Street of Knives
past pho shops and storefronts.
A woman sits in a doorway
with a child on her lap, her fingers
combing the scalp, picking out lice,
crushing them between her nails.
They say our middle world floats
between heaven and hell — they say
if you chant *Amitābha* ten thousand times
you will enter the Pure Land.
In the marketplace a flower stall is on fire
with orchids. Next to it
a butcher table with the smoked head
of a dog, and on the shelf
a large glass jar with a cobra
coiled in amber brandy.
Across the way in a storefront gallery
a man paints on a white canvas,
copying in exact pointillist detail Seurat's
Sunday Afternoon on the Island of La Grande Jatte.
The sky's drizzling a fine mist —
mua bui — rain dust.
You walk into a pho shop
where an old man ladles steaming broth into a bowl,
adds slices of raw beef as thin as onion skin,
some noodles, slivers of garlic, mung beans.
You squat on a stool a foot off the ground,
knees almost to your chin,
and watch a world pass by.
Two boys run down the road
holding each end of a paper dragon.

You know no one's name here, and no one
knows yours.
Wang Yang-ming said each person
has within — *liang-chih* —
"Buddha-nature," an intuitive
awareness of good.
You sit sipping pho
and try to work words into a notebook,
trying to make a poem.
A poet's duty, Nicanor Parra said,
is to improve on the blank page —
and doubted if it were possible.
A man walks by covering his head
with a palm leaf and carrying
in a small bamboo cage
a living scorpion.
What do you think will happen
if you run out of words?
Beckett said writing
is disimproving silence —
and went on to prove it.
The old pho man laughs,
opening his mouth,
and you see he has no teeth.
The humidity makes you drowsy.
Your mind floats away
to the Perfume River
and the Pagoda of the Celestial Lady
where boatwomen use their feet
to paddle the oars.
A kingfisher slices into the river
and rises with a silver fish
quivering in its beak.

Who was it that said
in some long-ago poem
this world is all we have
of paradise?

PART SEVEN

SEARCH FOR A MORAL ORDER

The Bridge of Change

Sausalito in the Sixties —
eight o'clock in the morning
at the No Name Bar,
John Logan with a double screwdriver
holding forth — today's subject:
Childhood and Tragedy —
the story of a boy
driving with his parents
over the Golden Gate Bridge,
the boy in the backseat,
parents up front
in a fierce argument.
Halfway across the bridge
traffic stalls to a halt,
cars bumper to bumper —
the mother throws open her door,
walks to the bridge railing,
looks back, looks again,
and jumps.
The son in the backseat,
father behind the wheel,
the bridge, the sea, islands in the bay,
a line of cars going nowhere.

Logan orders one more double,
a few hours away from standing
before his class at S.F. State
discussing Crane's adagios of islands,
the seal's wide spindrift gaze toward paradise,
and Hart's own leap
to no earthly shore —
students listening, rapt,
in the fluorescence of the room,
helicopters outside, riot police,
marchers carrying signs,
President Hayakawa in his office
phoning Reagan for the National Guard —
and on the other side of the world
B-52s carpet-bombing Hanoi.
Many years later, on the roof of a hotel,
Logan swayed before the railing, looking
over the glittering sea of the Tenderloin
(Was he drunk? Why did he jump?) — Logan,
who was born on a street named Joy,
who said in a poem, *I have no priest for now.*
Who will forgive me then.
Will you?
Outside the No Name Bar
fog streams over the Marin hills,
pours through the Golden Gate,
the bridge disappearing in mist,
like Crane's mythic bridge
blurring in a mist of words.
Logan stands before the bar
finishing his drink, ending the story
with his theory of poetry —
the poem as a bridge

connecting me to you,
you to me — poetry
in whose healing music we might trace
how to forgive, how to cross over,
making our long, difficult way
into grace.

What Holds Against Chaos

for Jerry Reddan

I am poured out like water
Psalm 22:14

Night on a tributary of the Amazon
shining lights over black water
searching for caimans
the reflections of their eyes
rubies lit from within

∾

*That the body of light come forth
from the body of fire*

∾

Carved on the rock walls at Red Rock
petroglyphs of a lost tribe
nobody alive can read them
one a spiraling galaxy
another of Kokop'ele with his flute
sounding a silent melody

∾

In the torque of a snail's shell
whorled proportions
of the golden ratio

∾

On Barbados
a white powdered beach
crushed shells of fossils
from the Cambrian Explosion

∾

Our mind is invisible
but the brain pulses with energy
neural synapses
weaving our thoughts
in a web of light

∾

Anamorphosis
of aurochs at Lascaux
Masked dancers
of Altamira
Magdalenian artists
Seventeen thousand years

∾

Zeno of Citium believed
a virtuous life was the point
of existence

∾

To build the city of Dioce
whose terraces are the colour of stars

∾

All summer a goshawk has hunted
among the pines around my cabin
All summer the dwindling families
of golden mantles and chickarees

∾

Nou goth sonne under wode

∾

Beckett said Joyce's work
is not *about* something
it *is* something

∾

In the Sonoran night
hunting with ultraviolet light
over the desert floor
scorpions come alive
in a luminous blue fire

∾

The rock walls of Cuzco
each stone set so carefully
perfectly
you cannot work a knife blade
between the cracks

∾

Experience is not the vision
Stan Rice said
The poem is

In the crown of a sunflower
seeds unfold
in Fibonacci numbers

Ubi sunt qui ante nos fuerunt?

Delautre at Vézelay
discovered
the secret of light —
a midsummer sun
through clerestory windows
illuminated terraces of fire
leading the eye to the Infinite

A neutrino
traveling at the speed of light
passes clean through
the inner galaxy
of our body
through molecules
through the sun system
of an atom
without impact
leaving no trace

When thou hast done
thou hast not Donne

∾

Summer solstice at Hovenweep
Winter solstice at Maeshowe
a dagger of light pierces
the center of all our days

∾

In Surprise Valley below Fort Bidwell
two sandhill cranes dance
next to a barn that's been collapsing
for a hundred years

∾

Nū scylun hergan   hefaenrīcaes Uard,
metudœs maecti   end his mōdgidanc

∾

Listening to a nightingale —
experience
"Ode to a Nightingale" —
vision

∾

From a Pisan cage
What thou lovest well remains
What thou lov'st well shall not be reft from thee

∞

In his room above the Spanish Steps
Keats knew he was dying
A flame moved
from one candle to another
as if a spirit
Lift me up he said to Severn
Don't be frightened

∞

Engraved in stone in a Roman graveyard
Here lies One
Whose Name was writ in Water

∞

That two atoms of hydrogen
will link with one atom of oxygen
is the precondition
for all we call
life

The Poem within the Poem

It is morning near a creek in the Sweetwaters,
the rising sun has lit up the tip of a cedar
and a man is sitting beneath it in a camp chair
drinking coffee and working over a poem.
From time to time he pauses from his task,
and looks at the world around him, listens
to the creek and birdsong of the forest,
watches a tiny nuthatch hop headfirst
down the trunk of a sugar pine, the only bird
that can perform such a feat. He goes back
to the poem, testing each word, working
his way down the page, making sounds,
mouthing syllables, a strange forest creature,
around him the resinous odor of pine
and cedar, and to the west a range of mountains,
an uplift of granite so immense, so massive
it can be seen from the moon. The man
is wondering about the end of his poem,
whether it should click shut, or open up.
The poem is not about sitting in a forest
on a summer morning — in it there is
a rainy night, and terror, there is an image
of a car speeding on a freeway in L.A.,
a teenager, driving very fast, crying, trying
to get home where his brother on the phone
had told him his mother is dying. The man
looks up from his words, watches the crown
of the cedar catch fire with the light
of the sun rising over Leviathan. A bee
blunders through the sage around him.
The boy had been at his friend's house,

listening to music — *Fontessa, The Golden Striker.*
The man wishes he could work those sounds
into his poem, something to place against
the boy's terror. The boy knows nothing yet
of true loss. Maybe this poem will help him,
the man thinks, hopes, as he looks up
at the great world around him, sees how
the sun has worked its way down the length
of the tree's trunk, how the whole cedar is now
sheathed in a blaze of light. The man is amazed
at this sight, and considers how he might use this
to guide the terrified boy on his drive home,
considers how there might yet be a luminous way
for him to end his poem.

Seventy-Five Years Old, Sitting with My Father

I've been sitting with my father again,
more and more these days as I approach
his age, as I come near the day of his death.
We sit together out back, under a sugar pine,
late afternoons mostly, the shadow time of day,
the sun's slanting light, the cliffs below Burnside.
I tell my father what I did that day, what amused me,
the things Miette said, the phone call from Kirby.
My father doesn't say much, which was his way in life;
now and then he will glance at me, and smile,
will tell me with a look to not be afraid, *it's true,*
he gestures, *the night is large, and the other dark*
is larger, it's like nothing you can imagine,
and I sit there looking up at the glowing cliffs,
dust motes, pollen ash, speckling the air around me.

Notes in Search of a Moral Order

I am haunted by memories.

A train ride in Thailand. A black Corvette.
Black-necked cranes of Druk Yul. The singing of the indri.

∾

In a Bangkok alley a dog is eating what appears to be its own entrails. Soldiers are milling around the courtyard of the Emerald Buddha. A few trash barrels are on fire, smudging the air with an oily smoke.

∾

I had been cycling the road along the East Fork of the Carson, past the Monitor turnoff, cottonwoods along the riverbank, fireweed, deep jade pools, autumn, a gold day in the high country, cycling past the convergence of the Carson and Silver Creek, when I came around a bend where two patrol cars, their lights flashing, were parked across the road, and a tow truck, its back end against the edge of the drop off, was winching a black Corvette out of the creek, up over rocks and boulders, water sluicing from the wreckage.

∾

Because I wanted more than could be given, I suffered. The oldest chapter of the oldest book in the world. In the great dzong at Punakha, I witnessed the Drametse Ngacham, a dance where the dancers wear animal masks: wolf, bear, tiger, dragon. They are danced in their peaceful forms, no wrath visages. It is said that witnessing this dance cleanses the spirit — the dancing removes all obstacles, each beat of the drums the dancers carry will bring liberation to everyone present in the courtyard. Perhaps. But I had come to Druk Yul, Land of the Thunder Dragon, in search of another dance, an ancient one from creatures who come down out of the sky.

∾

The cattle, large white brahmans, were milling around the tracks, some slumbering between the rails, a few dozen, humped shoulders, dark eyes, calm, peaceful creatures, rice paddies and small hills of the central Thai plain, egrets in the canals, full sun, humid, everything in a drowse.

∾

I found out later that he was nineteen and had stolen the Corvette in Stockton, racing across the San Joaquin up into the gold country, to Angels Camp, where a Highway Patrol pulled him over. As the officer approached, the young man floored it, and the chase was on, over Ebbetts Pass, down the steep winding road — and just past Scossas Cow Camp, he took a curve too fast, lost control, and launched into the air and down forty feet into Silver Creek.

∾

Bangkok was under martial law, soldiers massed at intersections, many of them almost boys, looking confused and frightened, the city sweltering in rage, hundreds of cars backed up, clogging the streets, horns blaring, crowds milling everywhere, some carrying signs, no one in control, the coup underway.

∾

I had been told about its singing. So I traveled to the Andasibe forest in search of the indri, the phantom creature of the canopy, who lives among air and light, whose singing, they say, opens a door to another world.

∾

On our long hike up to the Tiger's Lair, Kenlay, my guide, tried to explain the concept of *bey cha*, the aesthetic of performing everyday tasks gracefully, with care and consideration for others. In one of the meditation caves there was a statue of Padmasambhava holding the five-pronged vajra, symbolizing the transmutation of the five poisons — desire, hatred, ignorance, jealousy, pride. Before a statue of the Buddha, the wooden floor has been worn down into almost a human shape from devotees prostrating themselves. Some will do it one hundred thousand times. It takes two months. I stood there in the dark watching a monk kneel, then sprawl flat on his stomach, his arms forward as if diving into the lap of the Buddha.

∾

The express train from Bangkok to Chiang Mai, a straight track through the central plains, rice paddies, slow-moving rivers, cane fields, villages, and to the north, mountains, jungles with the last teak-bearing elephants. I was seated in the front coach behind a thick glass partition, the engineer on the other side, and I could see with him straight out to the track up ahead, the rails shining, canals and fields flashing past, and far off, where the tracks converged, a group of brahmans lounging.

∾

The sound of the chain ratcheting against boulders, the flashing lights, the sound of Silver Creek, the Corvette being winched up, coming out of the water, the body still behind the wheel, crushed in the wreckage.

They come in from the north, from Tibet, first just a few, then a dozen, and then more, the last of their kind, *thrung thrung karmo*, the sacred black-necked cranes, circling the Phobjikha Valley, their winter feeding grounds. When they land they begin their strange, gangly dancing, bowing and leaping — so the Great Circle comes around once more, completing itself, and all through Druk Yul the mask dances begin.

~

The engineer must have been drowsing, or daydreaming: he didn't sound the horn, he didn't stop — I couldn't believe what I was seeing, what was happening, as the train slammed into them at full speed, and the brahmans simply exploded.

~

I went to Druk Yul that I might see the black-necked cranes, before they are gone, before they disappear in the coming extinctions, with other creatures, other languages, dances, rituals.

~

They begin singing at dawn. High in the upper canopy. Facing the sun. Arms at their sides, hands in their laps, palms out, eyes half closed, as if in worship. The singing is unearthly. High-pitched, a kind of wailing, keening, but not sad. Haunting. The Malagasy say the indri are worshipping the sun, they are our ancestors, who never left the forest, and their singing is the singing of a father looking for his lost son.

Everything That Rises Must Converge

Late in life, in these last years,
I return to the City of Light
and stand at the tip of Île Saint-Louis
like standing on the prow of a ship
slicing through the Seine,
Notre-Dame rising behind me,
and behind it Sainte-Chapelle
with its chamber of stained-glass windows,
a Gothic vision of God's jewel-shattered heart.
Much of what I see now
I know
I am seeing for the last time.
On Pont Saint-Michel I watch
a young couple holding each other,
kissing, so much in love, so much
of their life ahead of them,
a tableau that seems to say
Forget the past, don't look back,
grab what is *now* — and yet I say
my past lives in me, augmenting
what is, and what is to be.
So I hold on
to the night gamelan of Ubud,
to the bells of the Minster,
the bells of Siena, Baeza, San Sebastián —
I hold on
to the vast inner space of Hagia Sophia,
the white plazas of Andalucía,
cloud country in the Valley of the Nidd,
the singing of the indri —
I keep in me

my room over the Campo dei Fiori
looking down
on the statue of Giordano Bruno
who believed time reveals
what is important in our lives,
what will measure the spirit.
What will Paris measure in me
this late in my life?
I walk through the D'Orsay,
the L'Orangerie, the Louvre,
I walk through the Etruscan room
with its statuary of smiling couples
lounging on the lids of their tombs,
I walk among the shattered gods
of the Greeks,
through the shimmering rooms
of Renoir, Monet, Bonnard —
I walk through the past, through history
with its singular moments of sorrow
and heartrending beauty —
I walk through
this Paris morning along the Seine
all my past burgeoning
undiminished
the way the bells sound in me
long after
they have stopped ringing.

Notes and Acknowledgments

My deep gratitude to the Lannan Foundation for their support, and to those whose critical readings and friendship have helped inform and encourage many of these poems: Ellen Scott, Kirby Wilkins, Rachel Harris, Bill Siverly, Rosie King's house-by-the-sea gang, Michael Hannon & Nancy Dahl, Jerry & Barbara Reddan, Peter Everwine, Charles Hanzlicek, Anita Barrows, Bill Mayer, Dan Gerber, Peter Weltner, Clem Starck, Charles Goodrich, Barbara Drake, Jerry & Janine Sprout, Tom & Melanie Meschery, Gary Young, Stephen Kessler, Christopher Buckley, and Michael Wiegers, my editor, along with all the good folk at Copper Canyon.

Thou Gavest It to Me from the Foundation of the World

> The title and italicized text are from the letters of Emily Dickinson.

Hózh'q

> A Navajo word for the beauty, balance, and harmony that can be found/created in our world.

Homage to the Makar

> Makar: an Orkney word for "poet."

Exchange

> In many countries of Southeast Asia, songbirds in small cages are sold near the New Year; the birds are ceremonially released to bring good luck for the coming year.

Animal Fair, 1950

> Chameleons: small lizards that were once sold at county fairs; they are not true chameleons, but anoles; like chameleons, they can change the color of their skin.

Copa

"Copa: The Hostess of the Inn." In some circles this poem is attributed to Virgil, though it resembles nothing else he has ever written (which is why Helen Waddell, the great Latin scholar and translator, believes he *did* write it). Others attribute the poem to Propertius or Cynthia. The various inns that lined the roads into and out of Rome were a combination of inn, tavern, and brothel.

Tu Fu: Eight Poems

These translations depend absolutely on David Hawkes's *A Little Primer of Tu Fu* (The Chinese University Press, Hong Kong).

The Breeze from Malabar

These versions are derived from the scholarship of Daniel H.H. Ingalls (*Sanskrit Poetry*, Belknap Press of Harvard University Press) and George L. Hart (*The Poems of Ancient Tamil*, University of California Press).

Passage

The epigraph from Dante translates as:

Guiding us was a voice that sang beyond the flame;
we gave it our rapt attention,
and came forth from the fire where the ascent began.

Passing Through: A Stroll at the End of the Twentieth Century

Theodor Adorno — "To write poetry after Auschwitz is barbaric" ("Cultural Criticism and Society," 1949).

And yet...and yet: from a haiku Kobayashi Issa wrote on the death of his daughter:

Yes the world of dew
is a world of dew
and yet...and yet

If You're Travelin' in the North Country Fair
A line from Bob Dylan's song "Girl from the North
Country."

La Doncella *of Llullaillaco*
In 1999, Dr. Johan Reinhard and his archaeological
team were traversing Andean mountains looking for
Inca sky-sacrifice sites. On the peak of the volcano
Llullaillaco (22,000 feet), they discovered a small
chamber that contained the perfectly preserved
mummies of three children, who had been there
for more than 500 years: *La doncella* (the maiden),
a fourteen-year-old girl; *La niña del rayo* (lightning
girl), six years old, who had been struck by lightning
some years after her death; and *El niño*, a six-year-
old boy. Child sacrifice, capacocha (*qhapaq hucha*),
was an important part of the Inca religion, used to
commemorate significant events or as an offering to
the gods in times of famine. In 2008, on a trip through
Argentina, I happened upon the Museum of High
Mountain Archeology, in the city of Salta, where on a
rotating basis the children are displayed in a climate-
controlled cubicle. It was there I encountered La
Doncella, in a sitting position, head slightly lowered,
looking as if she were alive and merely sleeping. I was
deeply moved; she seemed so utterly alone, and there
was something ghastly about it as well, about her being
on display for anyone to gaze at. Her presence haunted
me for many years, and it wasn't until I began to sense
her voice that the poem materialized.

accla: a sacrificial sun virgin.

coca & chicha: a mild narcotic and maize beer; scientific
analysis revealed the children had been drugged
for many days before the start of the climb and the
sacrificial ritual.

What Holds Against Chaos

Nou goth sonne under wode: Now goes the sun under the
woods

Ubi sunt qui ante nos fuerunt?: Where are those who
were before us?

These are the opening lines of Cædmon's "Hymn," the
oldest recorded Anglo-Saxon poem and the beginning
of English poetry:

Nū scylun hergan hefaenrīcaes Uard,
metudœs maecti end his mōdgidanc
Now we must honor the guardian of Heaven,
the might of the architect and his purpose

The Poem within the Poem

Fontessa and *The Golden Striker:* music composed by
John Lewis of the Modern Jazz Quartet.

Notes in Search of a Moral Order

Druk Yul: Bhutan, Land of the Thunder Dragon.

indri: the largest lemur of Madagascar and the
only one without a tail, thus giving it a humanlike
appearance. Babakoto is its Malagasy name. There are
numerous origin myths that claim an ancestral kinship
between the indri and humans. It is on the critically
endangered list.

Punakha Dzong: unique to Bhutan, a dzong is a fortress-temple building that houses administrative offices and monastic quarters, with large courtyards for religious ceremonies. Punakha, the former capital, is one of the twenty districts of Bhutan.

Drametse Ngacham: a Bhutanese sacred dance. In 2005, UNESCO designated the Drametse Ngacham as "an Intangible Cultural Heritage of Humanity." The dance celebrates the victory over evil and helps to remove suffering and its cause for all those present who witness its performance.

Tiger's Lair: Taktsang Gompa, Bhutan's famous monastery, perched high on the edge of a cliff overlooking Paro Valley.

Padmasambhava: one of the names of Guru Rinpoche, an important historical and religious figure in Bhutan, who according to legend founded Taktsang Gompa when he flew to the cliff on the back of a tigress to subdue a demon.

thrung thrung karmo: the Bhutanese name for the black-necked crane, derived from the sound the cranes make when they are dancing.

About the Author

Joseph Stroud is the author of six books of poetry, among them *Of This World: New and Selected Poems*, which was named by the San Francisco Poetry Center the outstanding book by an American poet for the year 2010. It was also a finalist for the PEN Center USA Literary Award, the Commonwealth California Book of the Year, and the Northern California Book Award. Stroud's other awards include a Pushcart Prize, the Witter Bynner Fellowship in poetry from the Library of Congress, the Award in Literature from the American Academy of Arts and Letters, and the Lannan Lifetime Achievement Award. He divides his time between a home in Santa Cruz on the Central California coast, a cabin in the Sierra Nevada, and a studio aerie in Puerto Vallarta, Mexico.

Poetry is vital to language and living. Since 1972, Copper Canyon Press has published extraordinary poetry from around the world to engage the imaginations and intellects of readers, writers, booksellers, librarians, teachers, students, and donors.

WE ARE GRATEFUL FOR THE MAJOR SUPPORT PROVIDED BY:

THE PAUL G. ALLEN
FAMILY FOUNDATION

TO LEARN MORE ABOUT UNDERWRITING
COPPER CANYON PRESS TITLES,
PLEASE CALL 360-385-4925 EXT. 103

Copper Canyon Press gratefully acknowledges the support of
Nancy Gifford for *Everything That Rises*

WE ARE GRATEFUL FOR THE MAJOR SUPPORT PROVIDED BY:

Anonymous

Jill Baker and Jeffrey Bishop

Anne and Geoffrey Barker

Donna and Matt Bellew

John Branch

Diana Broze

The Beatrice R. and Joseph A.
Coleman Foundation Inc.

The Currie Family Fund

Laurie and Oskar Eustis

Mimi Gardner Gates

Gull Industries Inc. on behalf of
William True

The Trust of Warren A. Gummow

Carolyn and Robert Hedin

Bruce Kahn

Phil Kovacevich and Eric Wechsler

Lakeside Industries Inc. on behalf
of Jeanne Marie Lee

Maureen Lee and Mark Busto

Peter Lewis

Ellie Mathews and Carl Youngmann
as The North Press

Hank Meijer

Gregg Orr

Petunia Charitable Fund and
adviser Elizabeth Hebert

Gay Phinny

Suzie Rapp and Mark Hamilton

Emily and Dan Raymond

Jill and Bill Ruckelshaus

Cynthia Sears

Kim and Jeff Seely

Richard Swank

Dan Waggoner

Barbara and Charles Wright

Caleb Young as C. Young Creative

The dedicated interns and
faithful volunteers of
Copper Canyon Press

The Chinese character for poetry is made up of two parts:
"word" and "temple." It also serves as pressmark for
Copper Canyon Press.

The poems are set in Verdigris Pro.
Book design and composition by Phil Kovacevich